Simple Solutions

to

Stress

GW00707766

By

Rose Saliba

Lapis Books

First Edition

© Rose Saliba 2009

Published in the UK by:

Lapis Books
27 Romany Close
Letchworth Garden City
Hertfordshire SG6 4LA

Tel: 07949 199222

www.lapisbooks.co.uk

The author gratefully acknowledges the contributions and support of family, friends, teachers, students and various organisations in the publication of this book.

ISBN 978-0-9547891-0-7

All rights reserved. No part of this publication may be reproduced, stored in, or introduced into a retrieval system, or transmitted in any form, or by any means (electronic, mechanical, photocopying, recording or otherwise) without the prior written permission of the copyright owner.

Printed in Hertfordshire

Contents

about the author

Rose Saliba, half Maltese and half Irish, is a professional Stress Management Trainer and Consultant. She has worked in this field for over 15 years, running courses for colleges, businesses, organisations and individuals.

She became fascinated by the subject, after attending a Stress Management Course at work. In researching this book she has tried and tested most of the techniques herself, gaining regular feedback from colleagues, students, family and friends.

She currently lives and works in London and Hertfordshire and runs a variety of courses and workshops.

Rose would love to hear your comments and feedback on the book and can be contacted through Lapis Books.

Introduction

by Rose Saliba

Thank you for buying my book of techniques for reducing stress.

I found that many of the selected techniques have been helpful on my own journey towards minimising the impact of negative stress in my life. I hope you will find some of them useful too.

Changing something small and practising it for a while worked best for me. Making changes little by little allows the body and the mind time to get used to new ways of being.

Stress is an inevitable part of life. Without it we would have no reason to get out of bed in the morning. It is part of our survival mechanism. If we are in danger, our stress hormones kick in to deal with the situation – by fleeing or fighting. If our stress levels remain too high, we may freeze and be unable to make a decision.

There are plenty of books written about what stress is and how to recognise it, so in this book, I am going to concentrate on **Simple Solutions to Stress** – ways to develop and maintain a **balance** between our positive and negative stress levels.

Anything that challenges or excites us is a positive stress. If we are scared, angry, bereaved, overworked, bullied, belittled or feel threatened in any way, we may experience negative stress. Too much negative stress can affect our health, if not addressed. Both positive and negative stress use energy, so it is important to find ways to **relax**.

One way we can lower our stress levels is by changing the way we think and feel. It is often the fear of something going wrong that can produce unnecessary stress.

Making any change in our lives creates a certain amount of stress. As we start to focus on reducing our stress levels, they may increase slightly, while we are learning new techniques – but the long-term benefits are worth it.

I hope you enjoy trying some of these **Simple Solutions to Stress**, increase your ability to relax and have more fun!

With love,

Rose

Signs of Healing!

When you first start to relax you will be releasing stored up tension and emotions from your body and mind. You might experience a variety of symptoms, particularly if you have been holding onto tension for a long period of time.

Don't be surprised if, for example, you start to feel uncomfortable or find tears flowing down your cheeks; you might develop a cold or a cough; you might find that you feel angry or sad more often; – these can be signs of release, a form of cleansing, of letting go, a 'detoxification' for the mind and body – all part of the healing journey.

It is worth persevering – acknowledge the feelings and work through them. You might find that you are able to laugh more easily and notice beauty around you, as you become more relaxed.

When choosing a Practitioner, check they are Professionally Qualified, affiliated to a Professional Organisation or Ruling Body, hold Professional Insurance and work within a Professional Code of Good Practice & Ethics.

Please note that if you are **pregnant**, some of the therapies and techniques in this book may not be suitable. Consult your doctor or a qualified practitioner.

how to use this book

There are several ways you could use this book to help reduce your stress levels:

♦ Turn to the Index at the back and choose the area you wish to know more about.

♦ Work your way from A to Z, skipping anything that does not appeal to you.

♦ Open the book at any page and try out the suggestion on that page.

♦ Flick through and see what catches your attention.

♦ Trust your own intuition.

♦ Enjoy the process.

Each section contains either a brief history or description of the stress reducing technique or therapy and a simple suggestion for trying it out. Look out for signs of healing and be patient with yourself.

Note: Words written in ***bold Italics*** indicate that there is a section in the book on that topic, which you will be able to find alphabetically, or from the index.

$\mathcal{A}$cupressure

Acupressure works by applying pressure to the 'acupoints' on the body (these are the same pressure points used for Acupuncture but without the needles). The points are found along our meridians (lines used in Chinese medicine which channel energy throughout our bodies). This system has been used in China for thousands of years and responds to bio-electrical impulses.

When we are stressed or in pain, the acupoints can be gently massaged to reduce tension and release the flow of energy.

Try this:

To relieve stress, anxiety and insomnia:

- Try a **Shiatsu** massage   or
- Gently massage the acupoint known as the *sea of tranquility** – which is three thumb widths up from the base of the sternum (breastbone) at the level of your heart. (*point CV17 on Conception Vessel)

To reduce cravings:

- Massage your outer ear and ear lobe

affirmations

These are positive statements aimed at changing our experience of life for the better.

We each have the power to choose how we think, how we react to a situation and what we believe. If we wish to change something in our lives, affirmations are a good place to start.

Constantly repeating a positive statement about yourself or a situation will bring about amazing changes. The statement will need to be positive, in the present tense (not the future or containing a negative) and have a ring of possibility about it.

You can write them down, say them aloud or to yourself, or even sing them.

Try it and see. Here are some examples to get you started:

- *I am calm and relaxed.*

- *I feel peaceful and rested.*

Alexander

technique

Developed by F Matthias Alexander and practised throughout the world, this technique works simply and effectively on posture, straightening our spines and aligning our bodies. Bad habits, such as crossing our legs, slouching when sitting, always carrying a handbag or a briefcase on the same side, can put our spine out of line and create stress in the body.

Try this:

at home:
Lie on your back, with your knees bent and your feet flat on the floor in line with your hips, ensuring your spine is straight and in contact with the floor. Use a small cushion or towel to support your head. Rest in that position for 10-20 minutes.

at work:
Consciously think about your posture whenever you can and straighten yourself when standing and sitting – uncross your legs and have both feet on the ground.

Aromatherapy

Essential oils have been used throughout history for healing (= *therapy*) and creating a pleasant smell (= *aroma*). The body absorbs oils through the skin (diluted) and the aroma stimulates the nervous system via the nose.

In the late 1920s, the French chemist, Gattefossé, burnt his hand and plunged it into a bowl of lavender oil. His hand healed remarkably quickly and this led him to explore the healing properties of other essential oils.

There are several ways to use essential oils. They can be added to a bath, used in massage oil, heated in an oil burner or in a bowl of water on a radiator. The aromas can also be found in scented candles or incense sticks. Be guided by your own nose!

Caution: Always consult an expert before using with small babies or if you are pregnant. Most essential oils should not be used directly on the skin but diluted in a base-oil, such as almond oil.

The most popular essential oils for **reducing stress** are listed below:

Chamomile Roman - soothing for mind and body, helps sleep.

Geranium – calming in small quantities and good for relieving pre-menstrual tension.

Lavender – relaxing, aids sleep (generally safe for babies and pregnant women)

Neroli – said to be good for shock

Ylang ylang – calming effect, used for reducing anger, irritability, guilt and panic attacks.

Calming Tips

at home:
♦ relax in the bath after adding a few drops of your favourite essential oil

♦ safely burn a scented candle (NB do not leave a burning candle unattended)

at work:
♦ put a few drops of essential oil on a hanky or tissue and allow the aroma to calm you, whenever you feel stressed (avoiding contact with the skin).

Bach Flowers

Dr Edward Bach researched the healing power of plants and flowers in the 1930s. He categorised 38 individual negative emotional states and developed a remedy for each, believing that physical health and emotional well-being are strongly linked.

The individual remedies are still made up in the area where Dr Bach did his research (Oxfordshire) and can be found in little bottles in most health stores, where you will usually find a leaflet or book to help you make your selection. The flowers are preserved in a grape alcohol solution (tincture). Only a few drops are needed.

For Stressful Situations:

- Try **Rescue Remedy** – four drops in a glass of water or onto your tongue

- Mix up to six remedies, to help alleviate stressful emotions. Take as above.

- Consult a Registered Bach Foundation Practitioner (see useful addresses)

Balance

We all need a certain amount of stress to stay motivated and respond to a challenge.

It is when we are overloaded with stress that problems can develop. Creating **balance** in our lives will help us to deal with stress more effectively.

If we lose our balance, physically, we get dizzy or fall over. If we become out of balance emotionally, we may get irritable, angry or find it difficult to cope with life. Finding and maintaining balance in different parts of our lives will help to reduce the impact of negative feelings and unpleasant situations.

We need a balance between work and **play**. Increasing our leisure time and including regular **relaxation** sessions into our busy lives, can help tremendously. Finding enjoyment in our work can also create more harmony in our lives.

Balancing the Breath:
Count the number of seconds it takes to breathe in and to breathe out. Now try to get them the same – in balance.

Bathing

Water is a great healer. Relax in a warm bubble bath – add **aromatherapy** oils for extra benefit. Turn off the phone or switch on the answer machine. Play some relaxing music. Burn some scented candles (safely) and enjoy for as long as possible.

Bathing in the sea or in a pool can be therapeutic and excellent **exercise**, especially if you like to swim.

To reduce stress:

- ◆ Schedule some time in a busy week to relax and enjoy a warm bubble bath. Do this as often as possible. Then have an early night!

- ◆ If you usually have a shower, take the time to bathe instead.

- ◆ Go **swimming** at least once a week (try it instead of the **gym** – it can be more calming).

Beliefs

We need to know what our basic beliefs are. Do they serve us well, or hinder us? Many of our beliefs were taken on board when we were small children. Many actually belong to our parents, or teachers and are not really ours at all! If we don't know what our beliefs mean to us personally, how can we be sure that they are good for us?

Imagine you are in the attic of your mind and having a clear-out – which beliefs would you keep and which would you like to change?

Examine several areas of your life and see how they are affected by your current belief system. Have you misinterpreted some beliefs from childhood? For example, many of us believe that we are simply 'not good enough', no matter how successful we are and this can undermine us.

Re-examining beliefs:
Take some quiet time-out to focus on your beliefs and decide whether or not they are good for you. Do they need modifying?

Breathing techniques

Breathing slowly and deeply is the key to calming the nerves. Becoming aware of how we are breathing will help to change it.

The feeling of not being in control can cause stress. The one thing in life we can control is our breathing. Even if we have breathing problems, such as asthma or panic attacks, slowing down each breath we take (even for one minute) will help to make us feel calmer.

Try this:

♦ Simply breathe out fully, or give a sigh of relief, to reduce stress and tension in the body.

♦ Breathe out fully. Then breathe in slowly counting to 3 or 4, let the breath out again, to the count of 3 or 4. Continue until feeling calm.

♦ Join a Chi Kung/*Qi Gong* class, which focuses on breathing, calming techniques and gentle exercises.

Chamomile

As a herbal remedy, Chamomile is used as a sedative and a tonic. Essential oils are referred to in the **Aromatherapy** section.

In the past, **Chamomile** was revered by the Egyptians for its healing properties and used by the Greeks for fevers and pre-menstrual tension. The Anglo-Saxons regarded it as one of their nine sacred herbs.

Chamomile tea is ideal when you want to calm down or have trouble sleeping.

Save the teabag and use when cool as a compress over closed eyes to help reduce dark shadows under the eyes, or for relieving sunburn and eczema.

Helpful hints:

- Drink a cup of chamomile tea before going to bed for a good night's sleep

- Keep some chamomile teabags in your desk at work

Colours

The colours we wear and those surrounding us can affect our moods. Blue is generally thought to reduce stress. It has a calming affect and is used to treat tension, fear, palpitations and insomnia in colour therapy.

The complementary colour of blue is orange and the two are often used together to help reduce stress.

There are various forms of colour therapy around to try, including being surrounded by light in the appropriate colour for your needs. Note that each individual may respond differently so test it out for yourself or with an experienced colour therapist.

To reduce stress:

♦ Carry a piece of blue/sky-blue material in your pocket (a silk scarf works well). For a calming affect, hold it, wear it or put it where you can see it.

♦ Choose pastel colours for your walls, pale green or pale pink can be restful on the eyes.

Crystals

Crystals have great healing powers. They work on a vibrational level according to their chemical make-up. They have been used throughout history as charms and jewellery.

Each stone is **unique**. They can be found in all kinds of shapes and sizes – polished (tumbled stones) or rough. Most retailers will tell you if the stone is genuine or if it has been dyed.

You can keep crystals in your pocket, wear them as jewellery, leave them on your desk, by the bed or in your living room. A clear crystal, hung in the window, can act as a prism and produce a beautiful rainbow of colour.

Choosing a crystal:

♦ If you have a particular problem you might want to consult a crystal healer or get someone to choose one for you.

♦ See which one catches your eye, pick it up and see how it feels.

D*ance*

Dancing is a great way to unwind, release tension and reduce stress levels. It is good exercise and lots of fun. It can increase your social life and make you feel good. Dancing can also help with your fitness levels, flexibility and general suppleness.

You can **dance** on your own or with others.

It doesn't matter which kind of dancing you choose – jazz, jive, rock, ballet, tap, ceroc, ballroom, traditional, contemporary, trance, disco, salsa, flamenco, tango, Gabrielle Roth's Five Rhythms, folk, country, line-dancing or any other style – as long as you enjoy it.

Simple solutions:

♦ Join a dance class

♦ Go out dancing with friends

♦ **Dance** around your living room

Daylight

We are all aware of feeling better when the sun is shining. People **smile** more. We get a spring in our step. The sun has healing qualities (as well as being dangerous if you are over-exposed to it) and helps boost our immune systems. Sunlight helps the body to absorb vitamin D.

The condition known as SAD syndrome or Seasonal Affective Disorder can develop when people start to feel depressed in the winter months. Treatment for this is usually a variation of ultra violet light therapy, or you could simply go out more often in **daylight**.

Getting more light:

♦ *Spend more time out of doors*

♦ *Go for a walk in your lunch hour – even in the winter (use sun protection in the summer)*

♦ *Take a holiday*

De-Clutter

Being surrounded by chaos can be stressful. It makes it harder to think straight and interferes with the decision making process. It also makes it very difficult to find things when you want them – defeating the purpose of hanging on to them…

We often hold onto old clothes, books, tapes, even old newspapers – for many different reasons. Hanging onto our past is not healthy. It is fine to keep happy memories alive, but we need to let go of the rest. They can keep us stuck in the past. There are now people, books and programmes specialising in helping you to de-clutter. It can be an emotional journey.

Try this:

- Start with a small area and work on freeing it up. Be ruthless!

- Keep that area clutter free for a while. Then start on another one.

- Get help if you need it.

Diet

This does not mean "go on a diet" which can often create more stress. It means: look at your diet and consider making gradual changes to what you eat and drink over a period of time.

Think of the word 'Diet' to mean moderation rather than abstinence and *eat healthily*.

You could try increasing the amount of fresh fruit and vegetables that you eat, whilst decreasing fatty and sweet things. Also try reducing the amount of caffeine, alcohol and tobacco that you have in a week.

Take it slowly:

♦ Make one small change only and stick to it, until it becomes automatic.

♦ Eat a piece of fruit (or two) when you might normally be tempted to comfort eat cakes, biscuits, crisps, sweets or chocolate.

♦ Drink more water.

Drivers

Discover what it is that drives you. There are five main **drivers** or *motivators* that cause people stress and most of us experience one or more simultaneously, or even all of them at once. (Also see **beliefs**.)

Each 'driver' can be a quality in its own right but taken too much to heart, can become a stressor both for yourself and for those around you.

Perfectionism	*I must be perfect So must they. Everything I do must be perfect*
Pleasing people	*I must always please everyone else*
Go faster	*Everything needs to be done in a hurry*
Be Strong	*I must never show weakness or need or ask for help*
Try harder	*Nothing is ever good enough – I must always try harder*

Are these reasonable expectations?

Examine your drivers:

Do any of these apply to you? How do they affect your life? What could you do differently? Examine your **beliefs** and experiment with new ways of being.

eating healthily

Wherever possible, eat regular meals and make them as healthy as possible. Avoid heavy meals before exercise or bedtime. Make sure you eat a variety of foods and ensure you get a **balance** of all the essentials: vitamins, minerals, fats, protein, fibre and carbohydrates. (Also see section on **Diet**.) Cutting cut down on fast food will help reduce salt and sugar intake. Experiment with fast cooking instead, have a selection of healthy ingredients at the ready.

If you need to snack, do so on healthy options.

Try this:

♦ Take healthy snacks with you – fresh fruit, dried fruit, unsalted nuts, reducing the number of chocolate bars or crisps in a week.

♦ Choose a healthy lunch option at least once or twice a week

Note – some cereal bars are full of sugar, so check the labels.

emotional healing

The ups and downs of our emotions can influence our stress levels considerably.

When we experience strong emotions, chemicals are released into the bloodstream. These chemicals have different affects on the body and may take some time to clear.

If we are not feeling any emotions, this may be equally stressful. We may be unable to feel joy or pleasure if we are suppressing fear or anger. Feeling detached from reality can be a guide that some professional help may be needed in this direction.

Our emotions are a necessary guide to our basic survival. When we experience a strong reaction to something – it is often a sign that something needs to change, either internally or externally.

Getting *in touch with our emotions* does not mean we should go about having temper tantrums or emotionally 'dumping' on others. It is about observing our feelings, reactions and responses and reflecting on them constructively.

(Continued…)

We deal with our emotions in different ways, as we do with our stress levels. There are no right or wrong answers.

If you had never experienced pain – how would you know when it was absent? The same applies to tranquillity. **Emotional Healing** is about allowing ourselves to be fully alive without being overcome by unwanted emotional excesses. In other words, by finding a **balance** in our emotional lives.

Try one of these:

Breathe out fully, then breathe in deeply and out again. Do this for at least a minute, or until calm.

Join a workshop or a class that promotes discussions about emotional issues.

Read a book about Emotions and learn as much as you can about them.

When experiencing a strong emotion, try breathing into it and acknowledging it. Try not to react to it, simply accept that it is there. Note it down and reflect on it later.

Let go of tension with a sigh of relief.

Emptying the mind

A great deal of stress is caused by thoughts and worries rushing around in our heads. We may be sitting still but our minds are racing around in the past and the future. Consciously taking the time to be "in the present moment" can reduce the anxiety that an over-active mind often produces.

Focusing on the present can be done in many different ways. Observing what is happening around us right now – what can we see, hear, smell or feel? Noticing the position of our body, shifting if we are uncomfortable, acknowledging any feelings or emotions that come up without getting involved with them. Simply observing what is happening, and *letting it go* – known as "mindfulness" in Buddhist teachings.

Techniques to try:

- Sit quietly and focus only on seeing what is around you for three to five minutes

- Next, close your eyes and simply listen

- Practise *meditation*

- Learn to *quieten the mind*

ℰxercise

An excellent way to reduce stress. The fitter you are, the better you are able to cope with stress.

There are so many different ways of exercising, that there is really no excuse not to do it. Find a way that appeals to you and try it out. Make it a regular habit. About 30 minutes, 3-5 times a week is generally the recommended amount. Start slowly. Don't overdo it, or you are more likely to give it up. Make it a pleasure not a punishment.

Some suggestions:

aerobics	badminton	canoeing	climbing
cycling	*dancing*	football	*gym*
hockey	jogging	*pilates*	rugby
skiing	kick-boxing	skating	steps
tennis	martial-arts	swimming	*tai chi*
skipping	table-tennis	trampoline	salsa
stretching	rollerblading	*walking*	*yoga*

◆ *Pick something easily accessible that you can do regularly.*

◆ *Start slowly and gradually build up.*

foot Massage

Having your feet massaged is a wonderfully relaxing experience (also see **Reflexology**). There are plenty of massage oils and creams on the market – peppermint and lavender are popular for feet. These are cooling and have the added benefit of hiding foot odours whilst being refreshing and stimulating.

A gentle foot massage before bed can also help you sleep better.

Try one of these:

♦ Soak tired feet in warm or luke-warm water; dry them gently; rub foot massage oil (or any cooling or moisturising body lotion) into the feet. Enjoy!

♦ Get a friend or loved one who likes massaging feet to give you a foot massage.

♦ Invest in a foot spa and indulge yourself.

Fresh Air

There is no substitute for fresh air. Make sure you get as much of it as possible. Breathe out fully and fill your lungs slowly.

Oxygen is essential to keep us alive so it makes sense to inhale a fresh dose of it as often as we can. Never miss the opportunity to go for a walk or just sit outside – a great way to reduce stress.

Essential for reducing stress:

- Go out at lunch time.

- Sit in the park – especially in winter, breathe through your nose to warm the air.

- Walk in the park or round the block.

- Breathe in fresh air deeply, hold and release.

- Go outside as often as possible.

Fun

This is a part of life a lot of busy people seem to forget about. What is life all about if you are not having plenty of fun? Everyone finds fun in different ways. Find someone, or others who enjoy the same things as you. Or just do it!

This does not mean having fun at someone else's expense. **Fun**, **laughter** and **play** are all exhilarating and great stress release.

Lighten up your load:

- Have some fun on a daily basis.

- If out of practice, start with once a week!

- If you have forgotten how, try a few new things and explore different ways of having fun.

- Make a list of things you like to do and schedule them into your life.

*g*ently does it....

Be **gentle** with yourself! Don't expect everything to change over night. We have had years to build up stressful patterns so it will take a while to dissolve them.

Whatever area you decide to start on, allow time for gentle change.

That means start an exercise programme *gently*. Change your diet *gradually* (one thing at a time). Don't beat yourself up with extra criticism if you relapse into old habits or feel stressed again. Consider gentle ways to relax.

Some good tips:

- *Gently* massage lotion all over your body after a warm *aromatherapy* bath or shower.

- Allow yourself to make some mistakes and have a few relapses.

- Reward all progress, no matter how small.

Gratitude

Think of all the things in life you have to be thankful for and count your blessings! This is a lot less stressful than constantly complaining and reliving any negative experiences.

Feeling thankful for the good things life has to offer and appreciating the world itself can leave you with a quiet sense of pure joy – a calmness that will filter through and support you during difficult times.

You don't need to be religious to be thankful for creation!

Try this:

♦ Showing gratitude, whenever you get the opportunity.

♦ Thanking **nature** for its very existence.

♦ Replacing moaning with **positivity**.

♦ Feeling glad to be alive

♦ Enjoy watching the sunrise and sunset

gym

Many people consider that the gym is a great way to reduce stress as it combines exercise and sociability. If you go to the gym on a regular basis – maybe three or four times a week, check out how you feel afterwards and try not to overdo it. *Exercise*, like anything else, can become addictive.

There are conflicting views on whether or not lifting weights at the gym reduces stress, or increases it. Lifting weights, and the preparation required to do this, can have a detrimental effect on our ability to remain calm during the day, particularly when done first thing in the morning. (see *swimming*)

Helpful hints:

♦ Use the gym safely.

♦ Drink plenty of water.

♦ Monitor your own stress levels regularly.

♦ Have your exercise regime checked by a professional trainer – to suit you.

Herbal Teas &

Remedies

More and more people are turning to traditional herbal remedies and cures for minor ailments.

There are records of herbal remedies dating back to Babylonian clay tablets from 3000BC. Chinese herbal medicine has been practised for thousands of years and lists over 800 herbs with therapeutic properties. Other written records came from Egypt, Assyria and the Indian *Ayurvedas* (sacred writings).

Some well-known herbal remedies:

- ◆ **Tea tree** is used as an antiseptic.
- ◆ **Arnica** is good for bruises (orally).
- ◆ **Aloe Vera** is excellent for burns.

These remedies can be found in most high street chemists, in the form of lotions, teas, infusions, oils, creams and tablets. (Continued..)

Fennel / Peppermint tea, or **Star Anise** are helpful for indigestion. The teas can be sweetened with honey. A piece of dried Star Anise can be gently chewed (like gum) or allowed to dissolve for a while under the tongue. Discard after use.

For headaches or migraine, try **Feverfew** or **Lavender**.

Rosemary and **Lemongrass** can help with circulation, digestion and aching muscles.

Valerian can be helpful at times of emotional distress or mild insomnia (not for prolonged use).

Chamomile tea will help you to relax and get a good night's sleep. (See section on *chamomile*)

Rosehip is rich in vitamin C, which can help when coping with stress.

One step at a time:

♦ Try a herbal or fruit tea before bedtime.

♦ Reduce caffeine intake during the day by substituting tea or coffee with a herbal or fruit tea.

♦ Consult a qualified herbalist.

holistic approach

The **holistic approach** deals with the whole person, not just the presenting symptoms – exploring the root causes of an illness, as well as treating it. These may be emotional, mental, physical or spiritual. Tackling all four areas seems to have better results in the long term.

Often an illness can come back if we continue with all our bad habits and negative patterns. So if you have a physical ailment, you might also address your emotional well-being or mental attitude in life, (see **Affirmations, Beliefs, Emotional Healing, Homeopathy** and **Positivity**).

There are many books now available in libraries, bookshops and health shops that will give you all kinds of advice. The best approach, as with anything, is to see what appeals to you and try that.

Mind, body, spirit, emotions:

Choose which area you want to work on first and combine it with a relaxation technique.

homeopathy

Homeopathy treats a person holistically, using substances that have been diluted over and over again to strengthen their potency. The word originates from Greek words that mean 'same' and 'suffering'. It was founded in Germany by Dr Samuel Christian Hahnemann (1755-1843) and is based on *'treating like with like'*.

A good Homeopath will treat the causes as well as the symptoms, working back through your lifelong ailments – a bit like peeling an onion. There are about 2,500 different remedies in this system and potencies vary from 6c* for mild ailments to 30c* for more acute ailments, to 200c*, an extremely powerful dilution (* = dilution factor/strength).

Growing in popularity, homeopathic alternatives can be found for many ailments – the healing may take a little longer but can prove worthwhile if you have built up an immunity to, or suffer side affects from certain medicines.

Recommended:
 ◆ *Visit a qualified Homeopath.*

Imagination

Use your imagination to create an ideal situation. For example, if your boss gives you a hard time, imagine him or her being nice to you. Work on this until it actually happens. *The power of imagination is incredible.*

If you are going into a stressful situation, it can be very helpful to use this technique beforehand, which is often referred to as *Creative **Visualisation**.*

Imagine every little detail to start with – colours, smells, sounds, how you feel and then recreate it in your mind, concentrating on **feeling** relaxed and confident. Help it to happen the way you would like it to!

Try this first:

Imagine you are lying or sitting in a restful place. Actually think about what is around you, the smells, the sounds, the trees, the sea. Breathe deeply and enjoy the feeling of peace, remembering that you just created it and can recreate it again at any time.

Invent your own solution

Based on the assumption that only you can truly know what is best for you, devising your own solution to reducing your stress has got to be a good idea. Going for a quick cigarette or a quick drink does not count! Think of another one.

Experiment with different ideas for reducing your stress at home, at work and in life, generally.

Choose something from this book, or brainstorm some ideas of your own. Write down everything that comes into your head without worrying about what others may think. A great idea will soon appear!

Try this:

- Take five minutes to think about your very own personal solution.
- Close your eyes and see what comes up, as you breathe slowly in and out.

Journal

Writing a journal or diary can be very therapeutic in getting it all out of your system and onto paper. It can be very enlightening to read again at a later date and can put life and worries into perspective.

Alternatively, write down all your fears, anxieties and frustrations on a sheet of paper. Then tear them up into little pieces and throw them away, symbolically ridding yourself of unhelpful negativity.

Keep a *happy journal*. Write down all the good things that have ever happened to you and add to it every day.

Find a *balance* – for every moan you put in your diary, put something positive that happened. There are plenty, you just have to look for them. Record all the things you did successfully, no matter how small.

Try it out today.

- Write a few pages each day for the next few days and see how it feels.

Journey

No matter where you are going, stay calm. If the traffic is bad, the bus is delayed, or the train is cancelled, stay calm. Getting upset does not solve the problem and causes a lot of unnecessary stress. Take a book to read, or use your imagination to help solve the problem. Find ways to use the time productively or creatively.

Only you know whether you find journeys relaxing or stressful. So only you know the best way to cope with them for you.

Life is a journey.

Is your journey through life stressful?
What can you do to make it less stressful?
What can you do to make it more enjoyable?

♦ Relax and enjoy the ride….

♦ Embrace the unpredictability of life and its journeys.

♦ Remember – it is often said that the journey itself is more important than reaching the destination.

Know yourself well

This is crucial to reducing your stress levels. Everyone is different and has different things that cause them stress. The trick is to know exactly what it is that stresses you and then find ways to deal with it.

You might want to explore *why* something stresses you. Is it one of your **drivers** or some old **beliefs** that you no longer need? Is there something bothering you from the past, that you need to deal with?

Self-awareness is the key to living life to the full without an excess of unwanted stress – allowing for the fact that we need a certain amount of stress to stay motivated and feel challenged.

- *How does stress affect you physically?*
- *How does stress affect you mentally?*
- *How does stress affect you emotionally?*
- *How does stress affect you* spiritually?
- *How does stress affect your* behaviour?
- *How are your relationships affected by your stress levels?*

....And what can you do about it?...

(Continued...)

Strategies for reducing stress by getting to know yourself better:

- Discover as much as you can about your real self.

- Start with something simple – name 10 things that you like and 10 that you dislike?

- Take some time at the end of the day to think about how you felt about things that happened and try to work out why, and what you can do to change it, or change the way you feel about it.

- Always remember to be gentle with yourself and take it slowly

- Join a self-awareness course

- See a stress consultant

- Choose a relaxation technique from this book and practice it regularly.

- Getting to know yourself better will give you more control over your life – you will be able to make informed choices and decisions affecting your life.

- Only you know what is best for you!

Laughter

Laughter is an excellent way to reduce stress.

Laughing exercises your lungs, stimulates your blood flow and boosts your immune system. It reduces tension and helps put things into perspective.

Laughing can help you recapture your *inner child*. And there have even been claims that people have cured themselves of illness through laughter.

Did you know that children laugh more than one hundred times a day and adults often only laugh four or five, if at all?

Bring back Laughter!

- Go and see a funny film
- Watch a comedy programme
- Go to a Comedy club
- Have a laugh with some friends (but not at anyone else's expense…)
- Laugh at home for no reason (this can feel strange at first but cheers you up and lightens your mood).

Let it go...

We can become so familiar with our stress levels, that we may not even be aware of how stressed we are, and yet still find it very difficult to let go.

When we first start to relax, it can feel as if there is something missing. We want our stress back!

High stress levels can become addictive. Learning to let go is like any other skill, it takes practice and motivation, commitment and perseverance.

We can choose how we react to people and situations. I know this is sometimes easier said than done but make a start. Let go of the hurt and the resentment. Let go of the fear and anger. Breathe in *love*. Relax and let go of the tension and anxiety before it builds up to extremes. Let it go slowly, at your own pace. Both physically and emotionally – *let it go....*

Close your eyes and consciously relax every part of yourself, body and mind – let it all go.

Lists

If you find that fear of forgetting things is causing you stress, try making a list of things to do. Write down the thoughts rushing around your head before you go to bed so that you can stop trying to remember them. Keep a pen and paper by the bed. Then if your worries wake you up in the night you can write them down and forget about them.

Making lists can be great as a reminder. Get extra satisfaction from them by ticking off actions once they are done.

If you discover that writing lists is causing you more stress, then tear them up!

Simple suggestions:

♦ Keep a notice board for your lists.

♦ Have a wipe-board in the kitchen or office so you can rub off the lists when they are done.

♦ Try prioritising the actions on your list, including relaxation.

Love

Feeling loved is an excellent way to reduce stress. Giving love is often difficult for people who don't feel loved. But the more you give out, the more you get back – though not always from the same direction.

If you look at all the self-help books on the market you will see most of them tell you to start by loving yourself. Try it! Loving yourself means being gentle with yourself, taking care of your needs, learning to relax and let go of the hassles of the day, spoiling yourself now and again, treating yourself to something nice. In fact, treating yourself the way you would like to be treated by someone who loves you.

The Simplest Solutions:

- *Start now. Be good to yourself.*
- *Start now. Forgive and move on.*
- *Start now. Enjoy life to the full.*
- *Start now. Love conquers all.*
- *Feel and give love all around you.*

$\mathcal{M}$assage

There are so many different kinds of **massage** to choose from – have great **fun** finding the right one for you. You could try an Indian Head Massage, a neck and shoulder massage or a full body massage – including **Aromatherapy** – using Essential Oils, or a **Shiatsu** – stimulating the **Acupressure** points.

Different types of massage involve varying techniques – and can be either invigorating or relaxing – so do check exactly what is involved before you book in for one. If you are experiencing discomfort during the session, be sure to let the Practitioner know. If you are going for an oil massage, remember that the oil is likely to soak into your clothes on the way home – so be prepared.

Afterwards, it is a good idea to relax quietly and drink plenty of water.

Simple solution:

♦ *Try one out for yourself. It's well worth it.*

Meditation

There are plenty of books, tapes and classes around teaching the art of **meditation**. It is the single most effective way to empty the clutter of the mind, relax the body and recharge your energies.

Get yourself into a comfortable position, sitting or lying down or even standing up. Try to make sure your back is straight and your arms, legs and feet are uncrossed. The key is to breathe deeply and slowly and focus your attention on something specific:

♦ *Listen to some relaxing music or a guided meditation.*

♦ *Follow your breath, in and out of your body.*

♦ *Focus on each movement as you walk or dance*

Start with just 5 minutes a day and build up.

Like everything, it takes practice. Be patient with yourself and enjoy the benefits...

Music

Whether you enjoy playing an instrument, listening, singing along or dancing to *music*, it can be a great way to de-stress and take your mind off things.

Music can be very therapeutic and is often used as a form of emotional therapy. Certain sounds are thought to have healing qualities, activating our chakras (energy centres). For example, the sounds made by Tibetan or crystal bowls are used in healing meditations.

The best style of music to relax to is a matter for individual choice. It is a good idea to listen to *Relaxation music* before buying it to see if it suits you. It might include the sounds of running water, birds singing, or subliminal messages (a form of hypnotherapy). Find something you like – then unwind to it.

Try this:

When you get in from a stressful day at work, put on your favourite CD and enjoy the music.

Nature

Nature usually has a calming influence on us, whether **walking** in the countryside, sitting in the park or paddling in the sea. Simply looking at pictures of nature can invoke feelings of **relaxation**.

Take time to appreciate the sky, the clouds, the sun, the moon, the stars, the sea, mountains, fields, trees, animals, birds, flowers, leaves and **fresh air**.

Simple solutions:

- Spend time in nature.

- Do some gardening.

- Listen to the birds sing in the morning.

- Stroke a cat.

- Take the dog for a walk.

- Hug a tree!

Naturopathy

Naturopathy is based on the body's ability to recover from illness, *naturally*. A naturopath will explore the causes of imbalance in the body using kinesiology (muscle-testing), iridology (study of the iris of the eye) and other means of examination.

Treatments may include detoxification, changing your diet, exercising, getting plenty of fresh air, ample water, day-light and relaxation. A naturopath may also recommend herbalism, **acupuncture**, **homeopathy**, **vitamins**, **laughter** and other therapies (many of which are mentioned in this book) that acknowledge the body's self-healing capacity and the healing power of **nature**.

Self help:

Start with your basic survival needs:

- **Air** *– how are you breathing?*
- **Water** *– are you drinking enough?*
- **Food** *– what are you eating?*
- **Movement** *– do you exercise?*

No!

(Learning to say no, nicely)

Always saying *'yes'* to things you do not really want to do, or have time to do, leads to resentment and stress. This can build up over time and make you irritable, or even ill.

Initially, saying *'no'* when you usually say *'yes'* takes practice and (be warned) may temporarily increase your stress levels until you get used to it, especially when you meet resistance from others. Practise.

There are many books, tapes and courses available on Assertiveness Training, Building Self-Esteem, Confidence Building, and Negotiation Skills, all of which are likely to have a section on Saying No! Courses are great for this as you get to role-play it (a safe way of practising your new skills).

Simple solution:

Practise different ways to say 'no', as nicely as possible. Reward yourself each time.

*ow....*

No matter how stressed you are feeling there is always something you can do about it. Try any of the techniques listed in this book. The most important thing to remember is to START **NOW**.

- ◆ Breathe out in a big sigh of relief. Then breathe in slowly, hold your breath for the count of two and release it slowly.

- ◆ Change your body posture to alter your mood.

- ◆ Have a positive thought.

- ◆ Repeat an **affirmation**.

- ◆ **Smile**!   ☺

- ◆ Sing!   ♫

- ◆ Do something nice for someone else…

- ◆ Do something nice for yourself…

Nurture Yourself

Make a point of looking after yourself well.

Living life in the fast lane often means skimping on good food and **exercise** and not allocating enough time to your own needs.

We only have one body and it is our responsibility to look after our body, soul, mind and emotional well being, so make sure you take good care of yourself.

The better you look after yourself, the better you will be able to cope with stress.

Nurturing Suggestions:

◆ *Buy healthy ingredients*
◆ *Learn how to cook nourishing meals*
◆ *Find some enjoyable exercise*
◆ *Have some fun*
◆ *Pamper yourself in a relaxing bath*
◆ *Have an early night*

◆ *Book a day in your diary that is just for you and do something pleasurable you have been meaning to do for ages.*

Organise

Organise yourself, your time & your environment. A great deal of stress is caused through chaos – not having enough time, not being able to find important papers, feeling, living and working in a mess.

Take the time to get yourself organised. Get a regular routine going that includes time for **relaxation**, **exercise** and eating freshly prepared meals. Find a way to organise your paperwork and set up a system that suits YOU. Tidy up regularly. A clear space helps you think more clearly. Clutter promotes confusion and accumulates dust.

Try not to do everything at once. Take one area in your life that causes you stress and re-organise it. Get help if you need it. Maintain the new way of doing things for at least 3-6 months to see a difference.

Re-organise your life!

- ◆ One step at a time….
- ◆ Have a clear out
- ◆ Tidy things away – everything needs its own place.

Osteopathy

From Greek words *osteon = bone* and *pathos = suffering* – Osteopathy is a healing system dealing with the structure of the body. Developed in the 1870s by Dr Andrew Taylor-Still, focusing on bones, joints, ligaments, tendons, muscles and connective tissue, with particular attention to the spine.

If part of the body is misaligned, it is often likely to have an affect on another part of the body, if not corrected. An Osteopath will re-align your spine or any abnormalities by manipulation or massage. This may sometimes be painful initially. One or more treatments may be necessary. NB *Ensure that the Osteopath is properly qualified.*

Suggestions to reduce stress:

♦ If you feel the slightest twinge – book in for a check up – the earlier the better.

♦ Remember – pain creates stress – and stress creates pain.

Outline your stressors

Try making a list of everything in your life that causes you stress and think of ways you can reduce their impact. There will always be areas we cannot change for the time being and so it is essential to develop ways of coping. It is often the way we *think* about something that makes it stressful. Can you change the way you see things? Is there a more positive way of looking at it?

Outline your De-stressors

Now make a list of everything that you do to relax, everything you enjoy doing. How many of these have you done in the last week or even the last month? Make a point of including at least one of these in your life within the next week/fortnight.

Try this:

*Spend one whole day, OK one hour then, when you do not complain at all about anything. Find something **positive** to say or think about instead. Then reward yourself with a special treat.*

Out with tension

We hold most of our stress and negative emotions in our bodies. This creates tension, which accumulates. If tension in the body does not get released, it can develop into aches, pains and illness (dis-ease).

An excellent exercise to release tension is to breathe in, hold your breath and tense up a part of your body, then release on the out-breath. Start with your toes or head and work all the way up and down the body. This is very effective as an antidote to insomnia. It is known as active progressive muscular relaxation.

You cannot hold tension in your body while you are breathing out. So make a conscious effort to *BREATHE OUT* fully, as often as possible. Breathe in slowly and deeply and as you breathe out say to yourself *"I breathe out tension and relax."*

Stop if you feel dizzy and breathe normally.

Try this:
Breathe out fully in a sigh of relief and feel your body relax. Great to do in traffic jams!

Own your

Opinions

Losing track of who we are, causes us a great deal of stress and anxiety – we may have the feeling that something is not quite right, or that something is missing.

We all have a right to our own opinions and the right to express them, bearing in mind that everyone else has the right to theirs too.

If you are unsure about your own opinions, start to clarify them, allowing yourself the luxury of changing your mind when further information is available.

Developing your opinions:

A good place to start, is with your personal preferences:

- *What is your favourite colour?*
- *What kind of films do you like?*
- *What kind of music do you like?*
- *Where would you like to go on holiday?*

When confident, move onto subject areas.

Pamper yourself

The only person who can reduce your stress is you. So start by pampering yourself. This is different for everyone. Some enjoy a hot foamy bath with soothing music by candlelight, others a sensuous body **massage**. Treat yourself to something mildly extravagant, or even wildly extravagant, if you can afford it.

Fresh flowers brighten up the room and cheer the soul. Pampering could include chocolate, or ice cream (in moderation) or a trip to the cinema or theatre, a manicure, a new haircut – whatever makes you feel good.

Pampering suggestions for reducing stress:

- *Have a massage with aromatherapy oils*
- *Have a long soak in the bath*
- *Buy yourself a bunch of flowers*
- *Enjoy a day out*
- *Spend some quality time alone*
- *Watch a film in the afternoon*
- *Gently rub body lotion all over*
- *Buy expensive chocolates just for you*

Paint

Imagine yourself on a hill with an easel in front of you and a brush in your hand, painting a beautiful landscape. Feel the freedom of being outdoors and creative at the same time.

Painting can be very satisfying, even if you don't consider yourself to be *artistic*. Whether you choose watercolours, oils, acrylics or emulsion, covering a surface of any size can be very therapeutic, as well as relaxing and great **fun**.

Try one of these:

♦ *Experiment with mixing colours*

♦ *Get yourself a sketch pad*

♦ *Join an art class*

♦ *Express yourself or your emotions through a new medium*

♦ *Take a blank sheet of paper and fill it however you like*

Pilates

The Pilates Method was developed by Joseph Pilates who did a lot of work with dancers and performers in the 1920s. It was originally geared towards people's individual needs and has evolved over time into an extremely popular **exercise** regime, integrating mind and body. Many well-known athletes practise it, as it builds strength and is claimed to be effective in helping recovery from sporting injuries.

There are 8 key aspects associated with the movements:

- Relaxation
- Concentration
- Alignment
- Breathing
- Centring
- Co-ordination
- Flowing Movements
- Stamina

What can you do?

See if there is a class near you. Or try it at home with a video or book to guide you.

Play

Playing is defined as any activity that brings pleasure or provides amusement. Sufferers from excessive stress, or depression, may have been missing a sense of **fun** from their lives, for some time. They may find it helpful to get in touch with their inner child and start exploring their *playful* side.

What did you enjoy doing as a child? Dressing up? Building things? Using crayons? Rolling down hills in the grass or the snow? Juggling balls? Anything that takes you away from your daily routine is bound to be good for you. *Have a go!*

Even if you have no recollection of *playing* as a child, there is still time to start right **now**. Let go of the need to be perfect – and join in. You will find your capacity for **play** will increase, and the initial stress of joining in will subside.

Simple solutions:
♦ **Play** with your children.
♦ Arrange a night out with your friends.
♦ Go and see a **play**, if you would rather observe– as long as you are having **fun**.

Positivity

Positivity is looking at the brighter side of life – making the best of any situation, finding the good in people. Feeling thankful for life itself. It is a choice – the way you look at the world and the way you think, affects the way you feel.

This does not mean being *in denial,* or refusing to acknowledge a problem. Explore your thoughts. Do you go over and over past 'disasters', or anticipate rejection? Do you see the world, generally, as safe, or dangerous?

Our energy goes into whatever we focus on, whether it is positive or negative. Our thoughts and feelings create our inner world and influence our experience of the world around us. What is your world like? Is it full of gloom and doom, or happiness and light?

I am not suggesting that you ignore reality in favour of having your head in the clouds – I am encouraging you to *shift your perspective.*

If you try sitting in a park, or going somewhere to be completely alone and find you are still feeling stressed and have niggling thoughts that keep going through your mind – then perhaps the thoughts need to change…. *How do you do this?*

Start *now*. What are you thinking? Do you feel you should be doing something else? Do you feel restless? Are you criticising yourself? Are you criticising me, or someone else? Are you expecting the worst to happen? It's a myth that this makes everything seem better – it may even increase the probability of things going wrong! Will you enjoy it if it goes right?

We are creating our feelings with our current thoughts. What a responsibility! The power to makes things better is all ours.

We can *choose* the way we think.

Developing Positivity:

♦ *Observe and examine your thoughts. Are they helping or hindering you?*

♦ *Try changing the way you feel by altering what you are thinking.*

♦ *Have a go with **affirmations***

♦ *Look on the bright side of life*

♦ *Think positively!*

Question yourself

Questioning yourself, your thoughts, your beliefs and what drives and motivates you will increase your **self-awareness** and help reduce your stress levels in the long term.

Do you know who you really are? What keeps you going? What patterns are you repeating that stop you from being where you want to be? Are you blaming other people, the government, or the world in general for your current stress levels? Are you prepared to take responsibility for your own life?

Quick fix:

♦ There is no quick fix for this one as it is a life long journey and it starts here.

♦ Enjoy it. See it as a challenge.

♦ Don't try to change everything in one go.

♦ Learn to like yourself as you are now. If you want to change something, then work on it but still appreciate yourself as you are right *now*.

♦ Laugh about it!

Qí gong

Qi (or Chi) means 'life energy' in Chinese and Gong means 'cultivation'.

Qi Gong (sometimes spelt and pronounced Chi Kung) is a series of gentle exercises used to heal the body and mind by increasing the flow of qi/chi around the body and creating harmony within.

It took me a good twelve weeks to learn how to *'stand still like a tree'*. But it was well worth persevering. Qi Gong helps to:

- ◆ relieve stress
- ◆ strengthen your immune system
- ◆ improve circulation
- ◆ increase vitality

I would also add that it did wonders for my back and improved my posture!

To relieve stress:
Practice standing still with legs hip width apart, knees slightly bent, hips in line, back straight and arms slightly bent. Breathe slowly in and out. Hold position for three minutes and build up to ten.

Quieten the mind

This is essential to reducing your stress levels. The mind stays active when we are sitting quietly, or trying to **sleep**. The easiest way to quieten or **empty the mind** is to focus on something different. Watch the flame of a candle, listen to relaxing **music**, or look at a beautiful picture. Concentrate on one point straight ahead of you. Or try counting your breaths (see section on **breathing**).

Every time your mind wanders off to its busy track, bring it back to the focus point. Start again at *one* if you are counting, watch the candle flicker and **dance**. Listen to one particular instrument at a time.

It takes practice, like any new skill. When the mind is quiet, creative ideas will come to you. You will feel rested and able to carry on at a calmer level. You may be more productive. Solutions pop into your mind.

To quieten your mind:

♦ *Start with any of the above suggestions for only one minute a day and gradually increase the time to fifteen or thirty minutes.*

Reflexology

Reflexology activates the body's natural healing powers by stimulating the energy zones that run throughout the body. A reflexologist works by applying gentle pressure on the feet at the reflex points where each of the ten energy zones end. There are five on each side of the body and they also end in the hands. All the body's organs are located in one of these energy zones.

There are many good books available on the subject and having a complete session can be very relaxing. Many people have sessions regularly, once a week or monthly, to reduce their stress levels.

Reducing Stress:

- *Book a session with a qualified Reflexologist and feel your worries dissolve as they treat your feet*
- *You can do **Reflexology** on yourself, or encourage your partner to treat you*

Note: Extreme caution should be taken during pregnancy. Consult an expert.

Reiki

This is one that is close to my heart. It is a complete healing system using universal energy. The word Reiki (pronounced Ray-Key) is Japanese – Rei meaning 'universal' and Ki meaning 'energy' or 'vital life force' (see section on *Qi Gong*).

Reiki works by channelling healing energy through our *chakras* (energy junctions in the body that correspond with the endocrine system). A Reiki healer may work with hands on the client's fully clothed body, or just above it.

You can be lying down or sitting in a chair to receive **Reiki**. It is a very relaxing experience. This in itself can be healing, if that is what you need. And the good news is that anyone can do it. You can learn to do it yourself for self-healing or to heal others.

To try Reiki:

Check your local holistic centre or health food shop to see if there is a practitioner near you, or contact The Reiki Association or other body to find a qualified practitioner.

Relaxation

The only true antidote to stress is relaxation.

This can take any form you like. In fact it must be something you like for it to be relaxing. Choose something that does not involve work or effort. A stroll through the park, a warm bubble bath, watching the sunset, listening to **music**, lying down, putting your feet up.

Create a relaxing atmosphere with soft lighting and gentle music or a relaxation tape. Turn off the phone, and the TV. Lie on the floor, or sit comfortably in a chair, making sure that your back is straight. Uncross your arms and legs. Close your eyes. Slow down your breathing, gradually going deeper and deeper. Feel yourself sink into the floor, or the chair and enjoy that heavy feeling.

Stress reduction:

*Practise **relaxation** on a daily basis. Pick a time of day when you can **switch off** for ten to fifteen minutes, enjoy being quiet and recharge your batteries.*

Rescue Remedy

Rescue Remedy is useful to take if you have had a shock or are preparing for a stressful event. It is made up of the following five **Bach Flower** remedies and can be found in health stores or chemists:

Cherry Plum   good for keeping negative thoughts and fears under control

Clematis   helps to focus attention

Impatiens   for developing patience and overcoming irritability

Rock Rose   the *emergency* remedy – helps reduce fear and panic

Star of Bethlehem   aids recovery after shock or an accident – comforting

To try Rescue Remedy:
- *put four drops in a glass of water and sip*
- *or put two drops onto your tongue and think a positive thought*

Self-awareness

A great deal of our stress is caused by how we think, feel and respond or react to situations, so becoming more self-aware is crucial.

We need to know what triggers our emotions and how to handle them, in order to stay calm during stressful situations.

As we become more aware of the way our thoughts and **beliefs** influence our stress levels, we can begin to improve our quality of life by making small changes – by shifting our perspective.

Observing our feelings and behaviour in certain situations will help identify which external factors contribute to our stress. Being tired, hot, cold, or hungry, family situations, social events, crowds, traffic. Knowing our internal and external **triggers** can help us to reduce stress.

Developing Self-awareness:
Set some quality time aside to think about why, when and how you get stressed. Examine the times when you feel relaxed.

Shiatsu

Shiatsu is a Japanese word meaning 'finger pressure'. It has roots in both Traditional Chinese Medicine and Zen practices. The idea is to balance the body by moving energy around the meridians and releasing any blockages by gently massaging pressure points in the same way as with **Acupressure**.

You will need to wear loose clothing to experience a **Shiatsu** massage – which involves pressure being applied to your acupoints points, known as 'tsubos', and some gentle stretching to release blocked energy.

It can be both relaxing and invigorating and can trigger a powerful healing process. Leave plenty of time to 'recover' afterwards and drink plenty of water.

To Try:

Go to a qualified Shiatsu Practitioner.

Enjoy!

Sleep

Make sure you get plenty! There is nothing like a good night's sleep to keep the body and mind in **balance**.

If you suffer from insomnia or disturbed sleep you might like to try doing a **relaxation** session before going to bed. You could also try cutting out caffeine in the evenings and drink a **chamomile** infusion before bed.

I sometimes keep a notepad by the bed, so that if I wake up worrying about something, I can jot it down and then forget about it. I also use the note pad to write down any dreams that I remember.

How much **sleep** a person needs, varies for each individual. Having a regular routine is highly recommended. Changing sleeping patterns may take a few weeks to establish. We generally sleep in cycles, from light sleep to deep sleep and back again. Enjoy that feeling as you drift off. Sleep well!

To keep stress at bay:

♦ *Have an early night at least once a week.*

Smile

Smile as often as possible.

Just as **laughter** can reduce our stress and boost our immune system, smiling can do the same. Even when you don't feel like smiling, it is worth the effort to try. Moving the muscles around your mouth upwards towards a **smile** can certainly start to make you feel better.

When the sun shines, people **smile** more readily. Try smiling even when the sun is not shining. Make someone's day – treat them to a **smile**. Most people will **smile** back and feel better for it!

Smiling strategy for stress reduction:

Smile *right now! Go on!*

See how many smiles you can fit into a day!

Spiritual healing

There have been claims of miraculous healing since time began. There are numerous examples demonstrated throughout the world on a daily basis. Whatever you believe, spontaneous healing occurs. Many people put this down to a form of **spiritual healing**. The basis for this could be your faith or belief system. If you believe it is possible, then it is.

Spiritual healing is part of the **holistic** approach, which involves mind, body, spirit and **emotional healing**. Each of these aspects of ourselves needs addressing to complete our healing, reduce our stress levels and prevent relapse.

Developing spiritual awareness:

Read some inspiring stories about people who have survived against the odds, about angels, about people's faith, their belief systems.

*Meditate; pray; reflect; spend time in **nature***

Swimming

Floating or gliding through water, propelled by the rhythmic movement of your arms and legs can be extremely relaxing and great **exercise**.

Both men and women have reported that **swimming** reduces stress and promotes **relaxation**. **Swimming** a few lengths in the morning, before work, at lunchtime or in the evening, can have a calming affect on your day.

Even if you are not a great swimmer, just being in the water can help. Water-aerobics are popular and do not usually require the ability to swim.

Salt-water is said to have healing properties and if you are nowhere near the sea, you could put a small amount of sea salt in your bath.

Swimming to reduce stress:

Make some time to swim in your busy week, take lessons if you don't know how to swim, or just float on the water.

Switch off

Switch off the phone, **switch off** the lights and **switch off** your mind.

Our over-active minds often run round and round in circles, increasing our stress levels. Any opportunity to **switch off** can increase concentration, creativity and energy levels. Productivity and performance levels tend to go down when people haven't had a break. Think how much more you get done physically, after you have had a rest. It works the same way for the mind.

If you find it difficult to simply **switch off** all those busy thoughts, try **meditation** or focusing on something different.

Sitting in front of the television doesn't count. Try switching that off for a while too!

Try this:

- Sitting quietly with your eyes closed.
- Counting your breaths up to ten (a full in and out = one). If you get distracted, start again at one. Keep going for as long as you can. *Enjoy switching off!*

T'ai Chi

T'ai Chi, also known as T'ai Chi Yuan, originated from China in the 13th Century when a Buddhist monk adapted martial arts techniques to the more relaxing, gentler movements of **Tai chi** in order to promote **balance** in the mind and body.

The slow, graceful movements and postures are combined with **breathing techniques** (Chi Kung or **Qi Gong**). They work well together to reduce stress and find **balance** physically, mentally and emotionally.

This form of gentle **exercise** is practised daily in China, often in town squares or wherever there is space for a crowd to gather. It is available in many colleges as a class and there is likely to be one near you.

It works by ensuring the smooth flow of energy (chi) along the meridians (energy lines) and creating **balance** within.

Try this:

- *Joining a T'ai Chi class*
- *Getting a book or video on it and try it out*

*t*ake a Break

No matter what you are doing, it is always a good idea to break for lunch. Even if you do not wish to eat a meal, you would benefit from eating something and definitely from taking a break – going for a walk or just away from your desk or whatever you have been doing.

Research has proved that concentration improves if you **take a break**. People who work through their lunch hour usually make more mistakes and are less productive in the afternoon than those who have had a break.

Take a Break

♦ Try taking a break in the middle of the day, even if it is only for 15 minutes;

♦ getting away from your desk and eating your lunch outside whenever possible.

♦ If you are not used to having a lunch break, maybe start with a short walk.

*t*ime

Management

Setting time aside for essential self-nurturing and self-maintenance is crucial for managing your stress levels. Put that together with some good organisational skills and you have the recipe for a full and active life with plenty of **relaxation** time scheduled into it.

Whether you feel you never have enough time or have too much of it, like everything else, it is about finding a **balance** – creating the best way for you. Spend a few days observing exactly how you spend your time. It could be enlightening. What are you avoiding by keeping so busy?

The important thing to remember is that your life is **unique** to you and how you chose to live it, is up to you.

Managing your Time:

♦ *Prioritise your priorities*

♦ *Make time for you and your own goals*

Triggers

Triggers are factors that generate stress. There are two main categories of **triggers**: *internal* and *external*.

Our *external triggers* are often out of our control but we need to be aware of them and take measures to reduce their impact on us – whether it is being too hot, cold, tired or hungry; family events, social occasions, work situations, commuting to work, meeting new people or just 'other people'.

It is our *internal triggers* that create stress about our external ones. It is what we believe or think about a situation that influences our stress levels – the expectation that something might go wrong. These unhelpful thought patterns increase our anxiety levels. Worrying needlessly is a waste of energy and creates a lot of extra stress in the body.

Simple Solutions:

♦ *Take time to think about your triggers*
♦ *Examine your thought patterns*
♦ *Explore ways of reducing their impact*

Understanding
yourself and others

Once you have got to know yourself and developed a compassionate understanding for your way of thinking, behaving and relating, you might like to explore how others see you and you see them.

Take time to really get to know people. To discover what makes them tick, what makes them happy, sad, *laugh*, cry, furious – and how you feel about it.

Sharing parts of yourself with others and trying to understand them is the key to satisfactory relationships.

Try this:

♦ Start with yourself – get to know your own likes and dislikes, *beliefs* and *values*.

♦ Discuss these with a good friend – discover how much you really understand each other. Make it fun…

Unique

*You are **unique**!*

Because you are **unique** – the things that cause you stress are unique to you. There may be similarities to others but it is your unique mind that determines your stress levels.

And…also, because you are **unique,** the way you de-stress yourself will be unique to you, too.

It is up to you to create ways to reduce your stress levels by changing the way you think about things that happen or might happen; the way you react to them and the way you see people and events.

You have a unique way of looking at the world, which you can adapt or change to your advantage. Your view of your world can be either stressful, or helpful and relaxing. It is your choice, your decision.

Try this:

- *Be your unique self and be happy!*

*V*alues

What is important to you? What do you care about in life? What are your **values?** Do you value yourself?

Sometimes when we find it stressful making a decision, it may be because we are not clear about our **values**. We may be trying to fit our lives around other people's values and priorities. This will generally make us unhappy without knowing why.

In the same way that we spring-cleaned our **beliefs**, it is crucial that we do the same with our **values**. Be clear about what they are and what they mean to you.

Advice on identifying what a value is varies from book to book but one thing is certain, our **values** and our interpretation of them are **unique** to each of us.

Clarifying your values:

◆ *Take time out to identify your values and check whether they reflect your true self.*

$\mathcal{V}$isualisation

Closing your eyes and imagining you are on a sandy beach or in a beautiful garden are excellent ways to practice both **relaxation** and **visualisation**.

It is also good if you are feeling too hot or too cold and can visualise the opposite. For example, if you are stuck on a crowded train or bus in the middle of summer, imagine you are playing in snow.

Visualisation can be used as part of the decision making process – by imagining what each choice will feel like. This involves seeing with your mind's eye and noting any physical or emotional response you may experience.

Visualising an interview or a difficult situation going well before hand is a very useful strategy. It is practising with your mind and often has the added benefit of getting positive inspirations at the same time.

Learning to visualise:
- *Practice during relaxation sessions*
- *Try it before an event to reduce stress*

Vitamins

Vitamin supplements have become increasingly popular in the battle for good health and a sense of well-being. If you have a balanced diet with plenty of fresh fruit and vegetables, you probably do not need to take extra vitamin supplements.

However, in times of severe stress we may deplete our bodies' vitamin reserves and may even have trouble absorbing vitamins and minerals into our immune system (especially if we have an on-going upset stomach). At such times, it may be beneficial to take extra supplements and seek medical or homeopathic advice for our symptoms.

There has also been a degree of controversy surrounding the B Vitamin groups of supplements. If you are taking anything in a mega-dose it stands to reason that this should be for a short period of time only and wean yourself off gradually as stopping suddenly after regular large doses can result in fatigue.

Only take vitamin supplements, as needed.

Walking

Walking is very good exercise, especially out in the fresh air. Brisk walking has the added benefit of being aerobic. Physical inactivity is thought to be one of the most common risk factors for heart disease, along with stress, smoking, high blood pressure and cholesterol. So it makes good sense to get moving as soon as possible.

Walking can be a great pleasure, whether alone or with others. **Walking** in **nature** or by the sea has a calming affect on our nervous system and stress levels. Again, each of us is different, so finding a way that suits you is the best way forward.

Start walking:

♦ Start by walking to work if you can, two or three times a week.

♦ Join a Ramblers club.

♦ Go for a walk at lunchtime – just round the block will make a difference.

♦ Use the walking machine in the gym.

Water

__Water__ is good for us in everyway.

Our bodies are made up mostly of water so it is crucial to replenish any water loss at every opportunity. It is recommended that we drink about 2 litres a day (not all at once!). This helps keep our skin moist and flushes toxins through the body. Drinking plenty of water assists the liver and kidneys in doing their jobs properly. This in turn helps our concentration and reduces headaches.

__Water__ has healing properties whether we drink it, bathe in it or look at it. It has both a calming and cleansing affect.

Water:

- *Check your daily intake of water.*

- *Spend some time by a lake, a river, a stream or by the sea.*

- *Take a long, relaxing bath or swim.*

Writing

Writing can be very therapeutic and an excellent way to reduce stress. If you get into the habit of writing down your stressful thoughts onto paper and then reading them back, you may find that they disappear and you are left wondering what all the fuss was about. Especially if you read them back three months later!

Many books recommend that you write a letter to someone you are angry with – this can be very useful as long as you DO NOT post it!! It can be very satisfying to burn it (safely) or shred it into little bits and feel your anger dissolve, reducing stress.

Writing a journal is an excellent way to keep track of your amazing progress (or you'll forget how stressed you once were!) and remind you of any techniques that worked for you.

Get writing:

Simply buy yourself a notebook or some notepaper and set some time each day to off- load your worries or write a poem.

X

marks the spot

- ◆ Starting here and now.

- ◆ There is no time like the present...

- ◆ Making small changes gradually for long-term results.

- ◆ Taking one small step at a time.

- ◆ Doing something **NOW**.

- ◆ Relaxing for ten minutes every day.

- ◆ Try again tomorrow if you missed today.

- ◆ There is really no excuse not to.

- ◆ Only you can improve your life.

- ◆ Only you can reduce your stress.

- ◆ You can do it!

oga

Originating from India, the word **Yoga** means "union" in Sanskrit (ancient Hindu writings) and there have been references to it since 3000 BC.

There are now numerous schools of yoga, mostly combining the physical postures (asana) with breath control (pranayama), encouraging unity between mind, body and spirit through various positions and stillness.

Yoga requires concentration, discipline and perseverance. Regular practice is said to give excellent health benefits and promote **relaxation** in mind, body and spirit.

Try this:

♦ Sample a few different **yoga** classes till you find one that suits you

♦ Practice the positions on a regular basis for maximum benefit

♦ Respect your limitations

You

Do you know the real you? Are you comfortable with who you are? What do you want out of life? What is important to you?

If you find yourself trying to please others most of the time or striving for approval, you may be creating stress for yourself. Not knowing what you want or who you truly are, can leave you feeling stressed without apparent reason.

Reflecting about *why* you do certain things, think in a particular way, or believe whatever you believe, will help you discover the real you. This may be uncomfortable to start with but will help clarify your perspectives.

Try spending some quality time alone, taking time to think, contemplate, plan, reassess, and be nice to yourself.

Remember:

- ◆ You are special
- ◆ You are *unique*.
- ◆ You are in charge of your life
- ◆ Only *you* can reduce your stress levels

Young

and Youthful

What is it that makes you feel alive and full of enthusiasm? What have you always dreamed of doing but never got round to, were too 'sensible' to do or thought was impossible?

Do you ever use your age as an excuse not to take on new challenges? Try doing something creative that you used to enjoy when you were a child or a teenager.

Laugh, **dance** and eat ice cream or chocolate (in moderation)! Experiment. Be **play**ful. Just imagine all the pleasures of youth with your newfound wisdom and less hormones….

Try this:

♦ *Wear something daring / colourful*

♦ *Play the **music** you loved in your teens. **Dance**. Go to a theme night. Organise a party. Dress up.*

♦ *Have **fun**.*

Zero Balancing

Developed by Dr Fritz Smith, an osteopath, physician and acupuncturist, in 1975, *zero balancing* combines eastern and western healing methods in a gentle hands-on approach using finger pressure and held stretches.

Treatments vary in length and are carried out fully clothed (wear lose clothing) lying on a massage couch.

Zero balancing works on your posture, weight-bearing joints and various energy points around the body.

Getting your body zero balanced regularly will help reduce stress, increase flexibility and improve your general well being.

Try this:

♦ *Find a qualified practitioner near you and book yourself in for a trial session.*

♦ *They usually recommend three sessions as a treatment. Try it out and see how it suits you.*

Z*zz zzz zzz...*

Making sure you get enough ***sleep*** will help to reduce the impact of stress in your life.

Try:

♦ Going to bed earlier regularly

♦ Getting plenty of good quality sleep

♦ Having an afternoon nap or a siesta

♦ Power-napping

♦ Having '40 winks' as often as possible

♦ Having an early night

♦ Doing a relaxation session before bed

Sweet dreams!

*e*pilogue

I hope you have found this selection of *Simple Solutions to Stress* useful and discovered some helpful techniques for reducing your stress levels.

Like any new skills, relaxation techniques and improved breathing and thinking habits, take a while to learn and require practice.

A certain amount of stress is inevitable – we are aiming to increase our tolerance to stress by developing our ability to deal with both our internal and external stressors.

It can be hard to let go of old habits – and stress, like any of our emotional states releases chemicals into our blood stream that we can become addicted to. We might even miss our stress levels at first…

Relaxation and slowing our **breathing** are the most effective antidotes.

Becoming calmer and achieving a balance, can lead to increased energy to spend on having fun and meeting exciting new challenges. Enjoy your journey.

useful addresses & websites

British Heart Foundation
14 Fitzhardings Street, London W1H 6DH
Heart information line: 08450 708070
www.bhf.org.uk

**British Association for Counselling and
Psychotherapy (BACP)**
BACP House, Unit 15 St John's Business Park
Lutterworth, Leicestershire LE17 4HB
Information Line: 0870 443 5227 (for information on
how to choose & Register of Qualified Practitioners)
www.bacp.co.uk

Dr Edward Bach Centre & Foundation
Mount Vernon, Bakers Lane
Sotwell, Oxfordshire OX10 0PZ
Tel: 01491 834678 (International Register of Qualified
Practitioners)
www.bachcentre.com

The British Complementary Medicine Association
www.bcma.co.uk

The Reiki Association:
www.reikiassociation.org.uk

The Shiatsu Society (UK)
Tel: 0845 130 4560
www.shiatsu.org

The British Wheel of Yoga
www.bwy.org.uk

For lists of professional bodies and associations try a
selection of websites.

Index